Section A Education

Topic 1 Explanations of the role and purpose of education

The role and purpose of education

Making sense of the role and purpose of education primarily involves understanding the **positive and negative sanctions** used in schools. The two **structural** perspectives of **functionalism** and **Marxism** are most applicable to this area of the syllabus and examiners will expect you to understand what factors they have in common as well as their contrasting views of the functions of education. They are both **macro** perspectives looking at the 'big picture' where education is a key institution in the **social construction** of society. Neither perspective pays much attention to classroom interaction, other than the work of Willis who provides a major critique of both perspectives, regarding them both as **over-deterministic**. Both functionalists and Marxists see students as '**cultural dupes**' or passive products of the education system when in reality they are not. Examiners will reward candidates who use one theory to evaluate the other, including the use of interactionism to criticise the structural approach. Practise this evaluative skill to gain AO2 marks. Examiners also like to see candidates applying sociological ideas and demonstrating an awareness of recent events. In a world of global economic competition education is always being discussed in terms of its role of generating a knowledge economy based on an educated workforce. The riots of 2011 raised again the debate about the role of schools in terms in reinforcing social control.

Read the extract and answer the following questions using your textbooks and notes.

Education is a key agency of secondary socialisation, reinforcing society's norms and values. All sociologists recognise the role of schools and colleges in offering **branching points** and the preparation of students for the world of work. Functionalists view the education process positively, arguing that it provides equality of opportunity as well as offering the necessary skills and instrumental values such as punctuality, attendance and respect for authority figures. In contrast, Marxists see education as a place where students learn to submit and know their place, particularly through the **hidden curriculum**. They challenge the idea that education is fair and equal, helping to promote a **meritocracy**. For Marxists class inequality is the prime determinant of educational success or failure. They see the education system in the UK as unjust, favouring those with money who either purchase a privileged education at a **private school** or finance a move to the catchment areas of good state schools. Functionalists would respond by saying that as education is provided for everyone, the successful ones are those who embrace this opportunity and work hard.

1 What process describes learning society's norms and values?

....

2 What term means every person having the same chances?

....

(40)

D1439458

3 What does the term 'cultural dupes' mean? `2 marks`

....

....

4 Explain what is meant by the term 'meritocracy'. `2 marks`

....

....

5 What is meant by the term 'branching points'? `2 marks`

....

....

....

6 Outline what is meant when functionalism and Marxism are described as structural theories. `6 marks`

....

....

....

....

....

....

....

....

....

....

7 Assess the claim that the hidden curriculum is predominantly a Marxist concept. Plan and write your answer on a separate sheet of paper. `20 marks`

Suggested plan

Introduction — defines term/s; states position/s to be argued

Define the term: 'hidden curriculum' refers to all that is learnt and internalised informally in school. Although an important Marxist concept, it is also recognised by feminists and functionalists. However, functionalists do not view it negatively, which Marxists and feminists do.

Main body — explains an argument/view, followed by counter-argument/view

Althusser describes education as an ISA transmitting hidden ideological messages that support capitalism. He argues that the hidden curriculum conditions working-class young people to accept social inequalities.

- AO2 point: functionalists would challenge this cynical and negative view, saying that schools seek the success of everyone.
- AO2 point: functionalists, in contrast to Marxists, see the hidden curriculum as largely harmless, reinforcing consensus values and helping to prepare students for the workforce.

Bowles and Gintis developed 'correspondence theory' to illustrate the way in which what goes on in schools 'corresponds' with the needs of the workplace. See hidden curriculum within schools as teaching students how to be passive and submissive to authority.

- AO2 point: the neo-Marxist Willis, while accepting the principle of hidden curriculum, demonstrates that it has no impact at all on his 'lads'.

Feminists are concerned about the negative and powerful impact the hidden curriculum can have in encouraging obedience and subservience. They have long argued that the hidden curriculum in school reinforces gender stereotypes and attitudes, including subject choices. The feminist Best suggests that females are underrepresented or stereotyped in textbooks, particularly in science subjects.

■ AO2 point: authors and publishers have recently made a concerted effort to portray female characters in books in a positive light.

Conclusion — summarises the answer to the question as argued in the main body

The hidden curriculum, while an important issue to Marxists, is also an issue of concern to feminists and functionalists.

Functionalist perspective on education

Read the extract and answer the following questions using your textbooks and notes.

The functionalist perspective on education derives to a large extent from the work and ideas of Emile Durkheim. He saw education as an important agency of socialisation promoting **value consensus** and turning children into '**social beings**'. He also saw education as a society in miniature and consequently viewed it as playing a crucial role in promoting **social integration**. This is done through socialising society's norms and values as well as encouraging children to respect each other and to work in groups. Talcott Parsons saw education as introducing and reinforcing **instrumental social values** and providing **functional prerequisites** (AGIL). Parsons also saw education as performing the important function of being a **bridge between home and work**. Functionalists see the education system as **meritocratic** by sifting and sorting students so that the most talented rise up to occupy the most functionally important roles society.

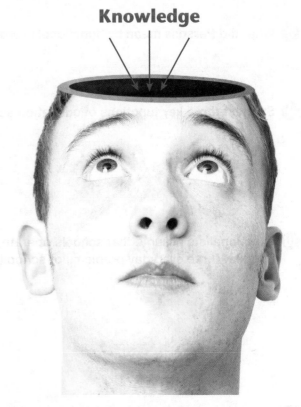

Knowledge

Fotolia

The functionalist view of education?

① **What do functionalists mean by 'value consensus'?**   `1 mark`

② **What term did Emile Durkheim use to describe the shared social values that education (and religion) can encourage?**   `1 mark`

③ **What is meant by 'social integration'?**   `1 mark`

50

4 What did Durkheim mean by the term 'social being'? `2 marks`

....

....

5 Suggest *three* universal values promoted by education according functionalists. `1 mark`

....

....

6 What criticism is being made about the functionalist theory in the image on page 5? `2 marks`

....

....

7 What is the function of knowledge according to Durkheim? `2 marks`

....

....

8 What did Parsons mean by 'functional prerequisites' (hint: AGIL)? `2 marks`

....

....

9 Suggest *three* key functions of education according to functionalists. `3 marks`

....

....

....

....

....

10 Functionalists assume that schools operate and reinforce value consensus. Suggest *three* everyday problems of schooling that functionalists ignore. `6 marks`

....

....

....

....

....

11 What did Talcott Parsons mean when he said education acted as a bridge between home and work? `6 marks`

....

....

....

....

12 Assess what is meant by equality of opportunity in education. Plan and write your answer on a separate sheet of paper. `20 marks`

Marxist perspective on education

Read the extract and answer the following questions using your textbooks and notes.

According to Marxists like Althusser, the main function of education is **cultural reproduction**, meaning that capitalist **ideology** is used to maintain the class inequalities of society. He describes education as an **ideological state apparatus** (ISA) whereby ruling-class ideas are dressed up as mainstream values that serve to hide the reality of the inequalities and unfairness of capitalism. Marxists argue that there is a history of working-class wastage of talent because the system is designed to fail them. This is achieved by factors like material deprivation, poor schools and teachers subjecting them to '**symbolic violence**' in the classroom. However, because of the ideological nature of education working-class students cannot see this. Instead they blame their underachievement on themselves through lack of ability, or effort, or a combination of both. Marxists call this process '**cooling out**'. Bowles and Gintis argue that a **correspondence principle** applies between the education system and the workplace.

35

1 What term do Marxists use to refer to the ideas that serve the interests of the ruling class?
1 mark

2 What is meant by the term 'cooling out'?
2 marks

3 What do Marxists mean by the phrase 'social' or 'cultural reproduction'?
2 marks

4 What does Pierre Bourdieu mean when he says working-class students are subject to 'symbolic violence'?
2 marks

5 Explain what Bowles and Gintis meant by the 'correspondence principle'.
2 marks

6 In what ways does the work of Willis challenge the ideas of Bowles and Gintis?
6 marks

7 What is meant when Althusser refers to education as an ISA? `6 marks`

....

....

....

....

....

....

....

8 Outline some reasons why Marxists are critical of the national curriculum. `12 marks`

....

....

....

....

....

....

....

....

....

....

....

....

....

....

....

....

....

....

....

....

New Right, selection and vocational education

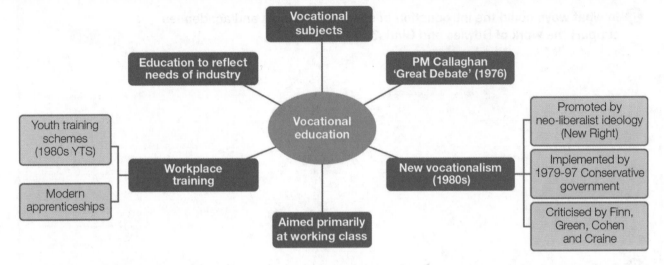

Examples of post-war vocational education.

Read the extract and answer the following questions using your textbooks and notes.

Ever since Prime Minister James Callaghan called for a 'Great Debate' on education in the 1970s the issue of vocational education has rarely been off the political agenda. The New Right Thatcher Conservative government of the 1980s introduced '**new vocationalism**' which included a range of training and education schemes. New Right/Thatcherism was less of a sociological approach than a neo-liberal political ideology that would be continued with Blair's New Labour policies. This neo-liberal view is that the reason for Britain's industrial decline is that schools and colleges have become divorced from the needs of industry, resulting in a skills crisis in the workplace. For the past 30 years there have been a range of policies and initiatives aimed at making education more vocational, such as the introduction of 'modern apprenticeships'. However, Marxists conclude that the real purpose of these vocational training schemes is to reinforce and legitimise class divisions and inequalities since they are primarily aimed at the working class, with the middle class still dominating academic and higher education.

(25)

1 Which sociological perspective is most closely associated with the development of 'new vocationalism' in the 1980s?   `1 mark`

....

2 What is the typical social class profile of those who do vocational education?   `1 mark`

....

3 What forms of vocational training were introduced in 1995 combining training in the workplace with part-time attendance at college?   `1 mark`

....

4 Why did PM James Callaghan call for a 'Great Debate' on education in the 1970s?

2 marks

....

....

5 In what ways could the introduction of specialist schools and academies support the work of Bowles and Gintis?

6 marks

....

....

....

....

....

....

....

6 Outline some of the reasons why Marxists are critical of vocational education initiatives like training schemes.

12 marks

....

....

....

....

....

....

....

....

....

....

....

....

....

....

....

....

....

Topic 2 Differential educational achievement of social groups

This area of the specification is a common subject of examination questions. The strongest candidates tend to be those who recognise differentiation and interplay between the three social groups **social class**, **gender** and **ethnicity**. For example if a question is about gender, you should recognise that middle-class boys and girls tend to have higher achievement levels than working-class girls and boys. In addition, ethnic group membership can influence the achievement of both girls and boys. The group 'social class' is recognised as the most important influence. According to Gillborn and

Mirza (2000) social class has twice the effect of ethnicity and five times the effect of gender on educational achievement. The other key aspect of differential educational achievement that examiners ask candidates to comment on and interpret is the debate over the influence of outside-school factors such as **material** and **cultural deprivation**. It is important that these are recognised as important factors, but they do need to be considered in conjunction with inside-school factors, which are addressed on pages 13, 19–25.

Social class

Read the extract and answer the following questions using your textbooks and notes.

Working-class underachievement, especially among those from homes where parents have semi-routine or routine (unskilled) occupations, has been explained by sociologists as stemming from a combination of **material deprivation** and **cultural deprivation** (lack of **cultural capital**) as well as some factors inside schools. Some have advocated **compensatory education** policies since these factors serve to reproduce existing inequalities and restrict **social mobility**, except for those who are highly motivated and ambitious. Britain has, according to the Sutton Trust (an educational charity) the worst of all worlds with regard to social class and education — **inequality of opportunity** with **inequality of outcome**. Politicians rarely talk about working-class underachievement as such, preferring to talk about the underachievement of the '**socially excluded**'.

1 Which sociologist is most closely associated with the term 'cultural capital'? `1 mark`

2 What is meant by social mobility? `1 mark`

3 Explain what is meant by the term 'compensatory education'. `2 marks`

4 Explain what is meant by the term 'socially excluded'. `2 marks`

....

....

5 Explain what is meant by the term 'inequality of opportunity'. `2 marks`

....

....

6 Explain what is meant by the term 'inequality of outcome'. `2 marks`

....

....

....

7 Why do politicians rarely talk about working-class underachievement, preferring to focus upon the 'socially excluded'? `6 marks`

....

....

....

....

....

....

....

....

8 Assess the view that that working-class underachievement in education is caused by factors outside school. Use this space to plan your essay and then write your essay on a separate sheet of paper. `20 marks`

....

....

....

....

....

....

....

....

Ethnicity

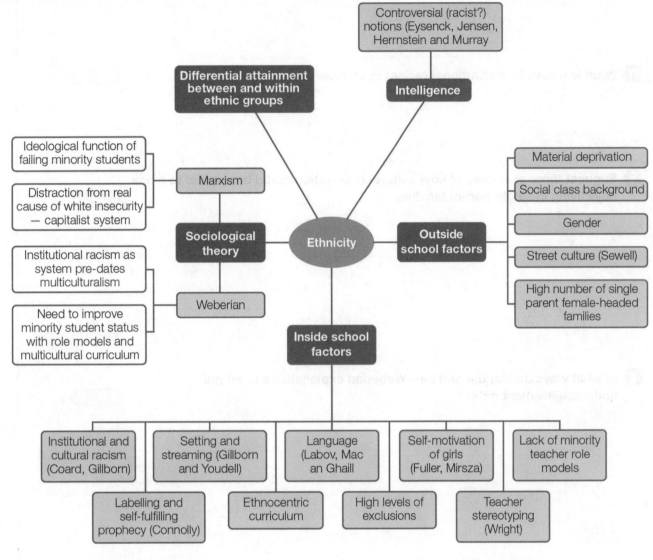

Controversial (racist?) notions (Eysenck, Jensen, Herrnstein and Murray

Intelligence

Differential attainment between and within ethnic groups

Ideological function of failing minority students

Distraction from real cause of white insecurity — capitalist system

Marxism

Institutional racism as system pre-dates multiculturalism

Need to improve minority student status with role models and multicultural curriculum

Weberian

Sociological theory

Ethnicity

Outside school factors

Material deprivation

Social class background

Gender

Street culture (Sewell)

High number of single parent female-headed families

Inside school factors

Institutional and cultural racism (Coard, Gillborn)

Setting and streaming (Gillborn and Youdell)

Language (Labov, Mac an Ghaill

Self-motivation of girls (Fuller, Mirsza)

Lack of minority teacher role models

Labelling and self-fulfilling prophecy (Connolly)

Ethnocentric curriculum

High levels of exclusions

Teacher stereotyping (Wright)

Key factors behind ethnic achievement.

Answer the following questions using your textbooks and notes.

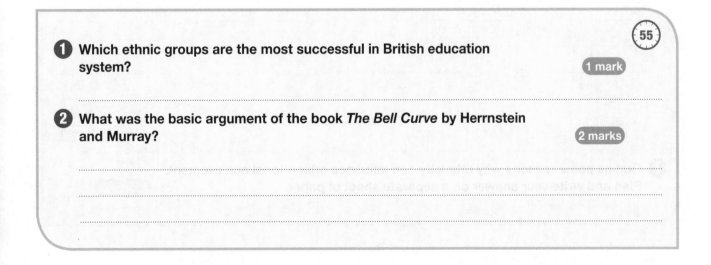

1 Which ethnic groups are the most successful in British education system?

1 mark

2 What was the basic argument of the book *The Bell Curve* by Herrnstein and Murray?

2 marks

55

3 What criticisms have sociologists made about Herrnstein and Murray's findings?

3 marks

....

....

....

4 What is meant by institutional racism in schools and colleges?

3 marks

....

....

....

5 Suggest *three* examples of how cultural deprivation could be applied to black boys living in single-parent families.

6 marks

....

....

....

....

....

....

6 In what ways do Marxist and neo-Weberian explanations of ethnic underachievement differ?

12 marks

....

....

....

....

....

....

....

....

....

....

....

....

....

7 Outline some reasons why ethnicity can influence educational achievement. Plan and write your answer on a separate sheet of paper.

20 marks

Gender

Read the extract and answer the following questions using your textbooks and notes.

Wilkinson talks of a '**genderquake**' with regard to recent changes in female student performance and the labour market. However, female success has not been universally welcomed. Warrington and Younger (1999) are critical of the way that the success of females in education has come to be seen as a problem for boys when, they argue, it should be a cause for celebration and congratulation. Many feminists also point to the fact that girls still attain more when taught in **single-sex schools**, suggesting that their wider achievement is in spite of the co-educational education system, not because of it. As a result of their success in schools and colleges, females are now entering higher education in ever-increasing numbers. Feminists would like to think that increasing numbers of female graduates will further extend the **feminisation of the workplace**. Females are now expected to infiltrate further into areas of work still currently regarded as 'men's work' (horizontal segregation) and to break through the so-called '**glass ceiling**' of vertical segregation.

1 **What has been the recent exam performance of boys and girls (improving or deteriorating)?**　　2 marks

....

....

2 **What does Wilkinson mean by a 'genderquake'?**　　2 marks

....

....

3 **What is meant by the term 'feminisation of the workplace'?**　　2 marks

....

....

....

4 **What is meant by the term 'glass ceiling' in the workplace?**　　2 marks

....

....

....

5 **Explain why girls generally do better in single-sex schools.**　　3 marks

....

....

....

....

....

....

6 Suggest *three* reasons why boys are underperforming compared to girls. `6 marks`

....

....

....

....

....

....

....

7 Suggest *three* reasons why feminists are still unhappy about the education system despite females outperforming males. `6 marks`

....

....

....

....

....

....

....

....

8 Assess the view that female achievement in education is caused by changes inside school. `12 marks`

....

....

....

....

....

....

....

....

....

....

....

....

....

Material and cultural deprivation

Read the extract and answer the following questions using your textbooks and notes.

One of the sad features about the situation of people who live in **material deprivation** is that they tend to suffer from multiple deprivations. For example, children who live in deprived neighbourhoods tend to be served by correspondingly poor schools that are located in the bottom half of published 'league tables'. One response to this situation has been the idea of **compensatory education**. This is an attempt to address directly not only the many issues of poverty but also the (controversial) idea that many children grow up in homes where there is **cultural deprivation**. Bernstein's concept of a '**restricted**' linguistic code is an example; he suggested that the '**elaborate**' linguistic code of middle-class homes reflects that of the classroom and textbooks, in contrast to households using his 'restricted' code.

50

❶ **Give an example of 'compensatory education'.** 1 mark

❷ **How can a family *not* experiencing material deprivation take steps to improve their child's educational attainment?** 2 marks

❸ **Explain what is meant by the term 'cultural deprivation'.** 3 marks

❹ **Suggest *three* examples of material deprivation.** 3 marks

❺ **What is meant by the terms 'restricted code' and 'elaborate code'?** 4 marks

6 In what ways does Bourdieu's concept of 'symbolic violence' support Bernstein's 'linguistic codes'?

6 marks

....
....
....
....
....
....

7 Suggest two criticisms of cultural deprivation theory.

6 marks

....
....
....
....
....
....
....

8 Outline some of the arguments to support the idea of cultural deprivation among the working class. Use this space to plan your essay and then write your essay on a separate sheet of paper.

20 marks

....
....
....
....
....
....
....
....
....
....
....
....

Topic 3 Relationships and processes in schools

This aspect of the specification is usually studied and examined in the context of explaining differential achievement through factors that lie *within* schools (as opposed to outside factors like **material** and **cultural deprivation**). While this area has been traditionally dominated by **interactionists** and **labelling theory**, do not overlook the fact that **neo-Marxists**, **feminists** and most recently **postmodernists** have all undertaken research into the impact of **teacher/student relationships**, **student subcultures** and the **hidden curriculum**. Note the AQA specification includes in this area 'the organisation of teaching and learning' which includes debates about what makes a 'good school'. It is also worth noting that the government's explanation for student underachievement lies primarily with underperforming schools and poor teaching. Examiners will expect you to show awareness that social policy on improving school performance and setting targets also falls into this area. Early research in this area focused upon forms of labelling and teacher attitudes, such as placing **stereotypes** and '**ideal types**' in teacher's heads to explain working-class underachievement. From the 1970s onwards feminists highlighted stereotype-ridden books, a male-orientated curriculum and sexist teaching. Clearly significant change has occurred over the past 30 years, but some feminists argue that girls' current achievement is still in spite of the system rather than because of it. With regard to ethnicity, many sociologists argue that schools remain racist institutions with many teachers holding 'racialised expectations'.

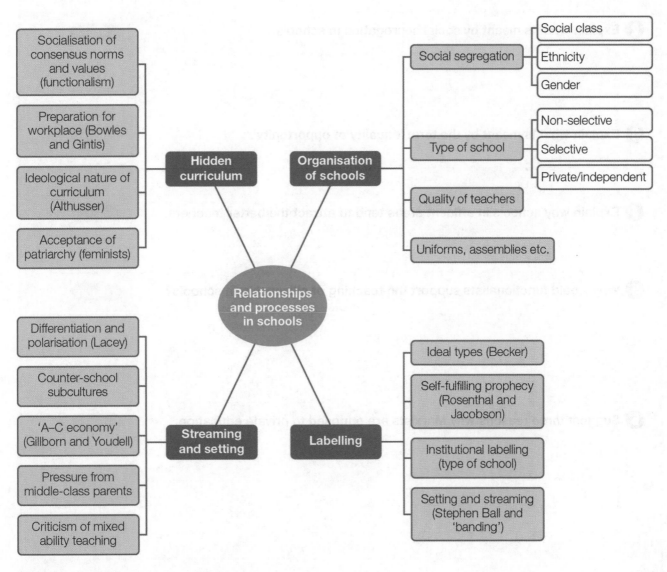

Different processes students are subject to in school.

The organisation of schools

Read the extract and answer the following questions using your textbooks and notes.

Schools are rarely truly **comprehensive** in their clientele and reflect some form of **social segregation**. The prevalence of **private schools** and variations in the quality of state provision means **equality of opportunity** is not a feature of the education system. While not all schools in deprived areas are bad schools, they often struggle to deliver high-quality education and achievement because of inadequate resources, high staff turnover and the difficulty of attracting **good teachers**, especially in key subjects like maths and science. The result is that a child's experience of education may mean putting up with an oppositional peer culture that bullies 'geeks' and 'boffins', endless supply teachers, run-down buildings and inadequate resources. The reality for schools now is that they have to engage in local turf wars in order to compete for their share of high-achieving students.

1 What is meant by the term 'comprehensive'? `1 mark`

2 Explain what is meant by social segregation in schools. `2 marks`

3 Explain what is meant by the term 'equality of opportunity'. `2 marks`

4 Explain why schools in affluent areas tend to attract the better teachers. `2 marks`

5 Why would functionalists support the teaching of citizenship in schools? `4 marks`

6 Suggest *three* reasons why Marxists are opposed to private education. `6 marks`

7 Outline some of the functions performed by school uniforms, assemblies, sports days and speech days.   9 marks

....
....
....
....
....
....
....
....
....
....
....
....
....
....
....
....

8 Outline how the hidden curriculum can impact on a child's experience of schooling. Plan and write your answer on a separate sheet of paper.   20 marks

Streaming and setting

Read the extract and answer the following questions using your textbooks and notes.

Many schools have reintroduced **setting** or **streaming**, effectively the '**banding**' of students, following criticism of **mixed-ability** teaching. One school in south London, in response to the fact that it is surrounded by **selective schools**, has subdivided itself into three 'mini-schools'. Each new intake of students is ranked on the basis of primary school performance and put into one of three mini-schools, each with a distinctive colour-coded uniform. Gillborne and Youdell researched what they termed the '**A–C economy**' and found one of the consequences was that middle-class and white students tended to be placed in higher streams compared to working-class or black students with the same measured ability. Streaming is often associated with **student subcultures**, with an elitist subculture in top streams and often a counter-school culture in the bottom streams.

1 Who studied the impact of 'banding' in the classic study *Beachside Comprehensive*?

1 mark

....

2 What is the difference between streaming and setting?

2 marks

....

....

3 Explain, with an example, what is meant by selective schools and colleges.

2 marks

....

....

....

4 Suggest two reasons why streaming and setting have become increasingly popular.

4 marks

....

....

....

....

....

5 Outline briefly why middle-class parents are generally in favour of streaming.

4 marks

....

....

....

....

....

6 What do Gillborn and Youdell mean by the 'A–C economy'? How do they argue that this impacts upon streaming?

4 marks

....

....

....

....

7 In his classic study *Hightown Grammar* (1970), Colin Lacey criticised streaming for encouraging both 'differentiation' and 'polarisation'. Briefly explain these two terms.

6 marks

....

....

....

....

8 Suggest *three* potential problems with mixed-ability teaching. `6 marks`

....

....

....

....

....

....

....

....

9 Critically evaluate the contribution of sub-cultural studies of classroom behaviour. `12 marks`

....

....

....

....

....

....

....

....

....

....

....

....

....

....

....

....

....

....

....

....

....

....

....

Labelling theory

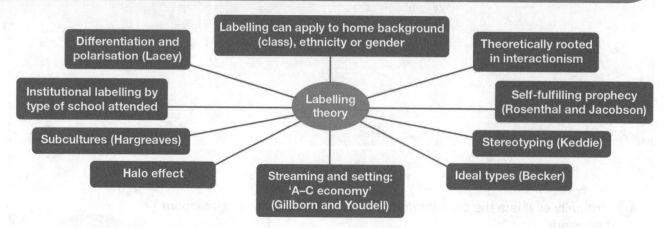

Key ideas about labelling theory.

Answer the following questions using your textbooks and notes.

1 What did Howard Becker discover in his study of 60 teachers? `1 mark` `35`

....

2 What important outcome did Rosenthal and Jacobson claim to show from
the labelling process? `1 mark`

....

3 What term applies to positively praising students and thus boosting their
confidence and motivation? `1 mark`

....

....

4 What educational process, in the form of internal selection, is accused of
labelling students? `1 mark`

....

5 How can allocation to sets or streams affect the identity of students? `2 marks`

....

....

6 Why was the tri-partite system accused of generating 'institutional labelling'? `2 marks`

....

....

....

7 What was the significance of skin colour in the eyes of teachers according to
Mairtin Mac an Ghaill? `2 marks`

....

....

8 How might students in bottom streams recognise that they have been labelled as 'destined to underachieve' by schools? `6 marks`

....

....

....

....

....

....

....

9 In what ways can labelling lead to a self-fulfilling prophecy? `6 marks`

....

....

....

....

....

....

10 What sociological evidence is there that labelling can be racist in schools? `12 marks`

....

....

....

....

....

....

....

....

....

....

....

....

....

....

....

....

....

....

Topic 4 The significance of educational policies

Education has been subject to government policies since the first Education Act (1870). This is partly due to political interference and partly to match education to the changing needs of the economy. The **1944 Education Act** supposedly introduced the concept of **equality of opportunity** through the universal sitting of the 11-plus examination. However, the system it introduced was seen as favouring the middle classes to such an extent that **private schools** went into decline in the 1950s. By contrast, the campaign for **comprehensive schools** in the 1960s and 1970s was supported by many middle-class families; children who failed the 11-plus exam had to endure the middle-class nightmare of the secondary modern school if parents could not afford to send their children to private school. In the 1970s a neo-liberalist (New Right) agenda came to dominate education; this eventually became part of government policy through the **1988 Education Reform Act**. This encouraged the **marketisation of education**, expressed most prominently through the principles of 'competition and choice'. The New Labour government maintained the neo-liberal policies but targeted the '**socially excluded**' through policies like **Sure Start** and **Excellence in Cities** (EiC). The Coalition government has put its focus upon **academies** and **free schools**.

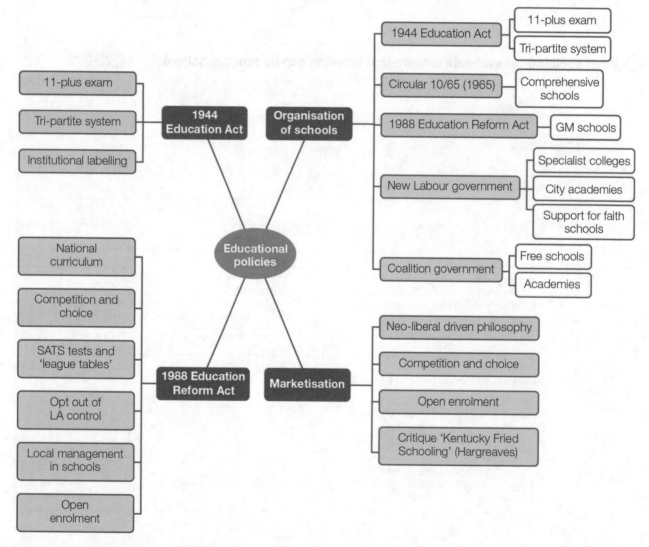

Educational policies since the 1944 Education Act.

Answer the following questions using your textbooks and notes.

(35)

1 What type of school did the Labour Government of 1964–70 encourage?   `1 mark`

....

2 What is the government-defined curriculum that all state schools in England are required to deliver?   `1 mark`

....

3 What are free schools?   `2 marks`

....

....

4 What are academies?   `2 marks`

....

....

....

5 Briefly explain the education system that was introduced with the 1944 Education Act.   `2 marks`

....

....

....

6 Suggest *three* criticisms of the system introduced with the 1944 Education Act.   `3 marks`

....

....

....

....

....

7 Identify *four* important measures introduced by the 1988 Education Reform Act.   `4 marks`

....

....

....

....

8 How was the New Labour initiative 'Sure Start' assumed to bring educational benefits?   `3 marks`

....

....

....

....

9 What was the Excellence in Cities (EiC) initiative?   `3 marks`

....

....

....

⑩ What is meant by the marketisation of education? `12 marks`

Exam-style questions on education

Read the extract below and answer Questions 01 to 04 on a separate sheet of paper—keep it with your workbook for reference.

A study from Edinburgh University has lent weight to claims that the comprehensive system has replaced selection by ability with selection by postcode. Poorer families have been priced out of the best schools due to soaring house prices in their catchment areas. They found that a child's schooling, whether comprehensive or grammar, made no difference to their prospects. Instead they found that the power of parental influence is much greater than anything schools can do. Middle-class children generally perform well in the education system, but even if they do badly at school, their parents, through their greater financial resources and social networks, help them secure higher-income jobs, allowing them to remain in their class of origin. Working-class students who did not excel at school were the biggest losers in the system.

01 Explain what is meant by the term 'cultural deprivation'. `2 marks` ② 2

02 Suggest three examples of material deprivation that could negatively impact upon educational performance. `6 marks` 6

03 Outline some of the reasons that explain how middle-class parents help their children perform well in the education system. `12 marks` 15

04 Using material from the extract and elsewhere, assess the view that Marxists see the role of education as 'reproducing the inequalities of society'. `20 marks` 25

Section B Research methods
Topic 1 Quantitative and qualitative methods of research

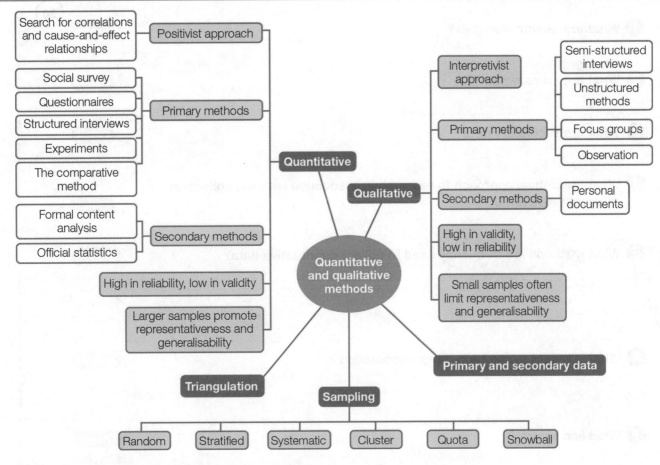

Key ideas about quantitative and qualitative approaches to research.

The purpose of sociology is to make sense of the social world we live in and understand human behaviour that takes place in that world. Because sociologists are social scientists their worldview has to be not only **rigorous** (established thoroughly and to a high standard) but defendable in terms of how data which support that worldview were collected. In addition, it must be **systematic** in its attempt to establish the truth about social phenomena. There are two types of data that sociologists can collect: **quantitative** and **qualitative**. The collection of data can be influenced both by the research method used (questionnaire, interview, observation etc.) as well as the theoretical approach adopted (**positivism**, **interpretivism**, **realism**). Both **primary data** and **secondary data** can take the form of quantitative or qualitative data. For examination purposes, it is essential to be able to differentiate clearly between the two.

Quantitative methods of research

Read the extract on page 30 and answer the following questions using your textbooks and notes.

An example of **quantitative data** is that collected by Callendar and Jackson (2004) who researched, using questionnaires, the extent to which future debt influenced a prospective student's decision whether or not to apply to university. The **target population** (all sixth formers) was surveyed through the use of a **sample** of 3582 drawn from a **sampling frame** of school sixth forms and FE colleges in England. The method used was self-completion questionnaires that were sent to educational institutions.

1 What are quantitative data? `1 mark`

2 What are primary data? `1 mark`

3 What are secondary data? `1 mark`

4 What theoretical approach to research is associated with the collection of quantitative data? `1 mark`

5 What methods are frequently used to collect quantitative data? `2 marks`

6 What is meant by the term 'target population'? `2 marks`

7 What is a sample? `2 marks`

8 What is a sampling frame? `2 marks`

9 What does the term 'representativeness' mean? `2 marks`

10 Why is it important for samples to be representative? `2 marks`

11 **Explain fully what is meant by quantitative research.** `12 marks`

....

....

....

....

....

....

....

....

....

....

....

....

....

....

....

....

....

....

Qualitative methods of research

Read the extract and answer the following questions using your textbooks and notes.

The qualitative approach is very different to the statistical data produced by the quantitative approach. It is more concerned with trying to understand, rather than measure and categorise, the social world. Its origins lie in the work of Max Weber, particularly his concept of *verstehen*, which means 'understand'.

Qualitative data is normally collected by **micro-sociologists** in relatively small-scale **ethnographic** research. Their goal is to understand the quality of people's lives in both detail and depth by gaining data that are as **naturalistic** as possible.

1 **What are qualitative data?** `1 mark`

....

2 **What theoretical approach to research is associated with the collection of qualitative data?** `1 mark`

....

3 What research methods are frequently used to collect qualitative data? `2 marks`

....

....

....

4 Explain what is meant by ethnography. `1 mark`

....

....

5 What are the commonest methods used in ethnographic studies? `1 mark`

....

6 What is meant by the term 'micro-sociology'? `3 marks`

....

....

....

....

7 Explain what is meant by the term 'naturalistic'. `2 marks`

....

....

....

....

8 Explain fully what is meant by qualitative research. `12 marks`

....

....

....

....

....

....

....

....

....

....

....

....

....

....

....

....

....

Topic 2 Sources of data

Questionnaires

Read the extract and answer the following questions using your textbooks and notes.

Social surveys are usually undertaken using **questionnaires**. This method is favoured by **positivists** since it is primarily associated with the collection of **quantitative data**. The data collected tend to be viewed as high in **reliability**. An example of research using questionnaires is that of Carolyn Jackson (2006) who undertook research into the behaviour of 'lads' and 'ladettes' in school. She designed a questionnaire comprised of **open** and **closed questions.** A copy of the questionnaire was given to every Year 9 student in two secondary schools in a town in north west England. The information elicited on the questionnaire was supplemented by interviews. Both research methods allowed respondents to **self-report** their own behaviour.

1 What is a social survey?   `1 mark`

....

....

2 What are closed questions?   `1 mark`

....

3 What are open questions?   `1 mark`

....

4 What does reliable mean in the context of research methods?   `1 mark`

....

5 What problems are there with postal or internet questionnaires? `2 marks`

....

....

6 Can questionnaires have an imposition factor or be biased?   `3 marks`

....

....

7 Give *three* examples of how quantitative data could be expressed in a visual form.   `3 marks`

....

....

....

8 What is meant by a self-report study? `4 marks`

....

....

....

9 Assess the strengths and limitations of using questionnaires as a research method. Plan and write your answer on a separate sheet of paper. `20 marks`

Interviews

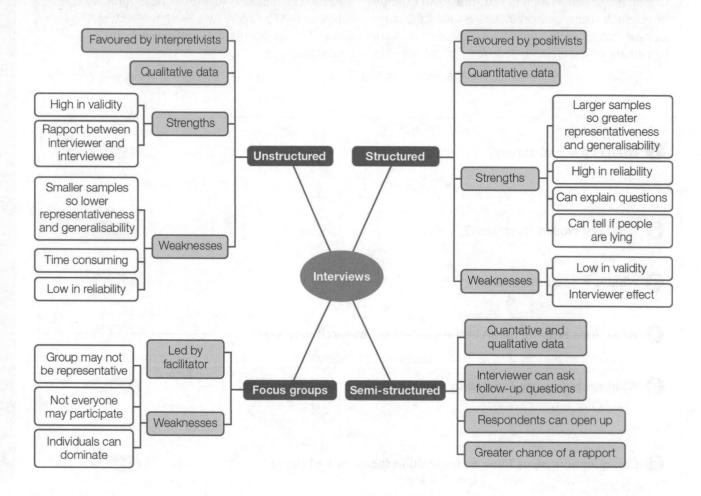

Different types of interview.

Answer the following questions using your textbooks and notes.

1 What type of interview could produce quantitative data? `1 mark`

....

2 What type of interview can collect both quantitative and qualitative data? `1 mark`

....

3 What type of interview is informal like a conversation?   `1 mark`

....

4 What type of interview involves a group of people?   `1 mark`

....

5 What type of data are collected from an unstructured interview?   `1 mark`

....

6 What is meant by the term 'rapport' in the context of interviews?   `2 marks`

....

....

7 What is meant by the term 'interviewer effect'?   `2 marks`

....

....

8 Apart from the interviewer effect, suggest *two* practical problems with conducting interviews.   `2 marks`

....

....

9 Assess the strengths and limitations of using structured interviews as a research method. Plan and write your answer on a separate sheet of paper.   `20 marks`

Observation

Read the extract and answer the following questions using your textbooks and notes.

Willis undertook an **ethnographic** approach to studying deviant boys in a Midlands comprehensive school. His primary method was **participant observation**. By gaining employment as a worker in the school coffee bar he was initially able to observe behaviour **covertly** without anyone knowing or suspecting that he was a researcher. Willis experienced both **practical** and **ethical** problems in the course of his research. For example, he was witness to many misdemeanours and acts of rule-breaking on the part of the 'lads'.

1 Explain what is meant by an ethnographic study.   `1 mark`

....

2 What type of data are normally collected by observation?   `1 mark`

....

3 What does the term 'covert' mean?   `1 mark`

....

4 What is the difference between participant and non-participant observation? `1 mark`

....

....

5 What sort of groups, if they are reluctant to take part in surveys or interviews, are often researched using observations? `1 mark`

....

....

6 What is the key benefit of doing covert research? `2 marks`

....

....

....

7 Identify *two* practical problems associated with covert observation. `2 marks`

....

....

....

8 Identify *two* ethical problems associated with covert observation. `2 marks`

....

....

....

9 What arguments might a researcher use to defend covert observation? `3 marks`

....

....

....

....

....

10 Why are observations often criticised in terms of reliability? `3 marks`

....

....

....

....

11 Why are observations often criticised for being unrepresentative? `3 marks`

....

....

....

12 Why is 'going native' a problem with participant observation? `3 marks`

....

....

....

13 What is meant by the 'Hawthorne effect'? `3 marks`

....

....

....

14 Assess the strengths and limitations of researchers using non-participant observation. Plan and write your answer on a separate sheet of paper. `20 marks`

Topic 3 The distinction between primary and secondary data

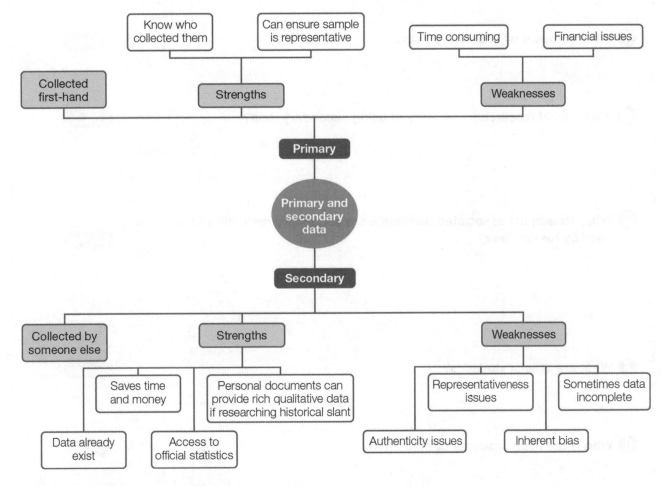

Key points about primary and seondary data.

Read the extract and answer the following questions using your textbooks and notes.

Angela Dale (2002) researched the unemployment rates of Pakistani and Bangladeshi women and found them to be significantly higher than other ethnic groups. Besides using focus groups to produce **primary data**, she also based her research on the **secondary data** she obtained from university entrance organisation UCAS. This was in the form of **statistics** on applications to higher education from Pakistani and Bangladeshi young people compared to other ethnic groups.

1 **What is meant by primary data?** `1 mark` `45`

....

2 **Give *three* methods that could be used for the production of primary data.** `1 mark`

....

3 What advantage do primary data provide to researchers? `2 marks`

4 What is meant by secondary data? `1 mark`

5 Why should researchers be wary of using secondary data? `3 marks`

6 Why, despite the associated problems, are secondary data still widely used by researchers? `3 marks`

7 What are official statistics? `2 marks`

8 Who is the main producer of statistics? `1 mark`

9 Why should official statistics be used with caution? `3 marks`

10 What is a formal content analysis of secondary data? `3 marks`

11 What is meant by the comparative method? `4 marks`

12 Assess the strengths and limitations of using secondary sources. Plan and write your answer on a separate sheet of paper. `20 marks`

Topic 4 Positivism, interpretivism and sociological methods

Positivism

Read the extract and answer the following questions using your textbooks and notes.

Positivists place a particular emphasis upon researching social behaviour that is directly **observable** and therefore **quantifiable** (for example, the number of marriages per year). Positivists argue that people's behaviour is shaped by observable '**social facts**' or structural factors that exist externally to the individual. The positivist approach is **objective** and **value free**. They look for **correlations** between social phenomena, such as the relationships between educational attainment and social class, gender and ethnicity. The ultimate goal of all positivists is to go beyond correlations and prove a **cause and effect** relationship.

1 What kind of data are collected by positivists? `1 mark`

2 Who undertook the classic positivist study of suicide? `1 mark`

3 What type of questions do positivists tend to ask? `1 mark`

4 Why do positivists argue that all research should be objective? `2 marks`

5 Explain what is meant by value freedom. `2 marks`

6 Explain what is meant by a correlation. `2 marks`

7 What is a cause-and-effect relationship? `2 marks`

8 What is meant by the term 'social fact'?

`2 marks`

....

....

9 What is meant by the term 'multivariate analysis'?

`4 marks`

....

....

....

....

10 Assess the strengths and limitations of adopting a positivist approach to research. Use this space to plan your essay and then write your essay on a separate sheet of paper.

`20 marks`

....

....

....

....

....

....

Interpretivism

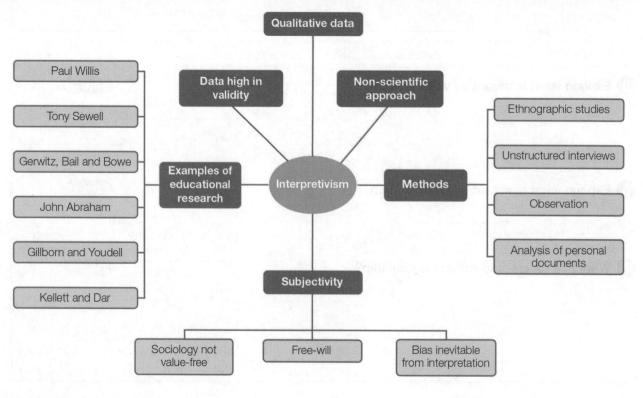

Key ideas about the interpretive approach.

Read the extract and answer the following questions using your textbooks and notes.

> The interpretivist approach tends to focus on meanings behind **social action** and is rooted in Weber's concept of *verstehen.* It mainly uses the primary research methods of unstructured interviews and observation. However, interpretivist sociologists can also use secondary data in the form of historical and **personal documents** as well as **semiotic analysis** of mass-media reports. This approach tends to be used by micro-sociologists, such as interactionists. Their research investigates everyday interaction, especially face-to-face behaviour such as that which may occur in the classroom between teachers and students or amongst students themselves.

1 Besides social action theory, by what other name is interpretivism known? `1 mark`

2 What kind of data are collected by interpretivists? `1 mark`

3 What problems are there with using personal documents in research? `2 marks`

4 What is semiotic analysis? `2 marks`

5 What is the main difference between interpretivism and positivism in the way they see human behaviour? `2 marks`

6 Why do interpretivists accuse positivism of being over-deterministic? `2 marks`

7 What did Weber mean by *verstehen*? `2 marks`

8 What is the significance of consciousness to interpretivist researchers? `2 marks`

....

....

....

9 How does the realist approach differ from both interpretivism and positivism? `6 marks`

....

....

....

....

....

....

....

10 Assess the strengths and limitations of adopting an interpretivist approach to research. Use this space to plan your essay and then write your essay on a separate sheet of paper. `20 marks`

....

....

....

....

....

....

....

....

....

....

....

....

Topic 5 Theoretical, practical and ethical considerations

Practical and ethical considerations

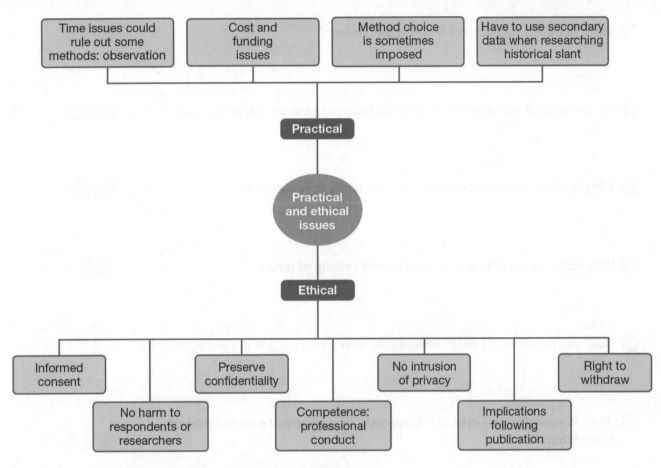

Researchers must take both practical and ethical factors into account.

Answer the following questions using your textbooks and notes.

40

1 **What are the two key practical problems of research?** 2 marks

....

....

2 **Can personal factors influence research?** 2 marks

....

....

3 **Do researchers always have full control of what methods to use?** 2 marks

....

....

4 Why might time constraints shape what method is used?   2 marks

....

....

5 How might researching a past era influence a research project?   2 marks

....

....

6 What is meant by the term 'informed consent'?   2 marks

....

....

7 Under what circumstances might informed consent be inappropriate?   2 marks

....

....

8 Why is it important to maintain confidentiality in research?   2 marks

....

....

9 Why might anonymity add to quality and validity of data?   2 marks

....

....

10 How can researchers avoid unwittingly identifying people in their research?   2 marks

....

....

11 What is meant by the ethical requirement of competence on the part of researchers?   2 marks

....

....

12 Do sociologists have any ethical responsibility with regard to how their research is used once it is published?   3 marks

....

....

....

13 Can respondents pull out of research, even at an advanced stage?   2 marks

....

....

14 Can the research topic raise ethical concerns?   3 marks

....

....

....

15 What should happen after the research is undertaken and before publication? `2 marks`

....

....

16 Why might forming relationships between researcher and respondent
prove problematic? `6 marks`

....

....

....

....

....

Theoretical approaches and sociological methods

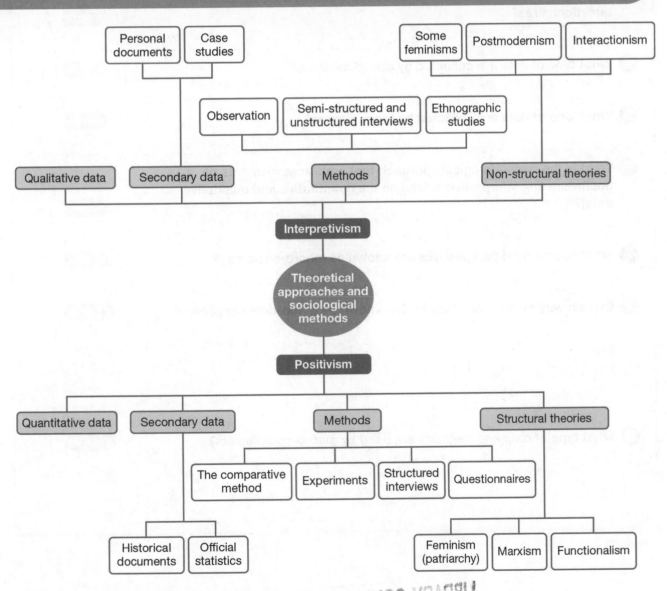

Although these approaches seem polarised, many researchers embrace both.

Read the extract and answer the following questions using your textbooks and notes.

Kelletth and Dar (2007) used a triangulation approach to research the links between children, poverty and literacy. They took the highly unusual step of using children as researchers; they wanted treat them as 'experts' of their own experiences. They also felt that children would gain higher quality responses from their peers than would be the case if adults asked the questions. The child-researchers were all volunteers and trained by university academics over a period of 12 weeks. The child-researchers used a combination of **questionnaires**, **interviews** and **focus groups.**

1 **What term means 'using a variety of research methods' as in the above study?** `1 mark` (45)

....

2 **What potential problems are there in researching children?** `3 marks`

....
....
....

3 **What type of methodological approach is primarily associated with questionnaires?** `1 mark`

....

4 **What type of data are collected by questionnaires?** `1 mark`

....

5 **What kind of data are collected by focus groups?** `1 mark`

....

6 **What is the methodological approach that embraces elements of positivism and interpretivism (and hence quantitative and qualitative data)?** `1 mark`

....

7 **What sociological perspectives are known as macro-sociology?** `1 mark`

....

8 **Explain why macro-sociology is also known as a 'top-down approach'.** `4 marks`

....
....
....
....

9 **What type of data and methods are used by macro-sociologists?** `2 marks`

....
....